ALIEN INVASION! THE COMPLETE GUIDE TO HAVING CHILDREN

Steven Appleby

THANKS TO ~
JO BAIRSTOW, GILLIAN SIMMONS, JONATHAN
BOATFIELD, LIZ CALDER, KASPER DE GRAAF, JANNY
KENT, GEORGE SKIPPER, CATHY HUSZAR, FRAN,
THE COTON PLAYGROUP MUMS & ALL WHO VOTED FOR
THIS BOOK ON THE BLOOMSBURY WEBSITE.

& VERY SPECIAL THANKS, AS ALWAYS, TO NICOLA FOR
BEING MY SPECIAL, INSPIRATIONAL, LOVING
PARTNER & FRIEND

THIS PAPERBACK EDITION PUBLISHED 1999
FIRST PUBLISHED 1998
COPYRIGHT STEVEN APPLEBY © 1998
THE MORAL RIGHT OF THE AUTHOR HAS BEEN ASSERTED

BLOOMSBURY PUBLISHING PLC
38 SOHO SQUARE, LONDON W1V 5DF

ISBN 0 7475 4455 7

PRINTED IN GREAT BRITAIN
BY BATH PRESS

For all my children.

I look forward nervously to
your inevitable revenge...

Love, Dad 13·07·1998

FAMILY CONTRACT
BETWEEN PARENTS & CHILDREN

We, your parents, declare that...

1 — We'll love you if you behave.
2 — We'll love you if you do what you're asked.
3 — We'll love you if you keep quiet.
4 — We'll love you if you go to bed and stay there.
5 — We'll love you if you do well at school.
6 — We'll love you if you help out.
7 — We'll love you if you don't show us up
      in front of our guests.
8 — We'll love you if you're a success.*
9 — We'll love you if you love us.

SIGNED:

‒ ‒ ‒ ‒ ‒ ‒ ‒ ‒ ‒ ‒ ‒ ‒

MUM & DAD.

* This clause applies to every walk of life while we're alive
and in perpetuity.

CONTENTS

The author and his wife
BEFORE CHILDREN: AFTER CHILDREN:

STATUS OF SEXLIFE: ACTIVE!   STATUS OF SEXLIFE: HIBERNATING.

INTRODUCTION

Having children is the single most traumatic, terrifying and life changing event most of us will ever experience – including death. Death comes and then it's over. Children last for the rest of your life.   Men will risk their lives as soldiers, racing drivers, mountaineers and even bus drivers rather than stay at home and change nappies. Having been turned down as a mountaineer, soldier, racing driver and bus driver they'll stand outside their house in the rain and dangerously SMOKE CIGARETTES rather than face up to their howling little responsibilities.
I know I do.
  Children are the proven major cause of ageing, heart disease, migraine, depression, disappointment, hair loss, grey hair, irritation, fed-up-ness, bad driving, bad breath and bladder problems.

  They suck out your life forces, including your money, until you're just a wizened husk. Then they leave home.
  NOW READ ON...

Would you like to come home with me?

Of course. I'm your husband.

THE BEGINNING OF ALL THE TROUBLE.

1
CONTRACEPTION!

At some point during normal – or abnormal – [†] sexual intercourse the MALE releases sperm which swim up the vagina of the FEMALE, find her egg and fertilise it.

At this point in the proceedings a tiny but immensely powerful signal is sent out from the female's womb across trillions of light years to the distant galaxy where the babies of all lifeforms are nurtured. A procedure is set in motion and nine months later[*] the baby arrives.

fig i – ONLY ONE SPERM REACHES IT'S DESTINATION OUT OF MANY.

START

Toilet. Hanky. Thigh. Sheet. Finger. Pyjamas. Egg. Knee. Floor. Pillow case. Stomach. Nose.

Some couples are more fertile than others, and many don't even have to physically touch in order to send the signal off to the vast listening computers which constantly monitor the skies of K-CAB 3.

fig ii – MIX UP! MRS X AND MRS Y GET GIVEN EACH OTHER'S BABIES.

SHRIEK!! Xpple zot! KKKKPT!! Gah!

[†] See my companion volume NORMAL SEX.
[*] The length of time it takes a spacecraft to travel from their galaxy to ours.

10

However, before you start planning for your own little alien's arrival, why not put your clothes back on and consider the pros and cons for a moment. Here are some useful charts and diagrams to help you make your mind up...

THINGS YOU CAN DO IF YOU DON'T HAVE CHILDREN. (Add your hobbies and interests to this column).	THINGS YOU CAN DO ONCE YOU'VE GOT CHILDREN.
1 - Lie in.	1 - Er...
2 - Pop over to Paris for the weekend on the spur of the moment.	
3 - Go to the cinema whenever you want.	
4 - Spend your money on yourself.	
5 - Sleep.	
6 - Watch the T.V. programmes you want to watch.	
7 - Wear clothes that aren't covered in baby vomit.	
8 - Keep the house tidy.	

Continue on a separate sheet if necessary.

THE FINANCIAL COST:

YOUR LIFE-STYLE

JOLLY NICE INDEEDY THANK YOU VERY MUCH!

WELL OFF.

COMFORTABLE.

POVERTY.

DEBT.

PRISON.

SINGLE. A COUPLE BOTH WORKING. 1 CHILD. 2 3 4 5 MORE...

NUMBER OF CHILDREN

A DIAGRAM SHOWING YOUR HORIZONS BEFORE & AFTER CHILDREN:

fig a - BEFORE   LIMITLESS.   HORIZON

The world is my oyster!

fig b - AFTER

Horizon closes in.

BUMP!

OUCH!

11

THE PSYCHOLOGICAL COST:
Children cause headaches...

THE TEMPORAL COST:
Time flies...

SOME ADVICE ON HOW TO AVOID HAVING CHILDREN...

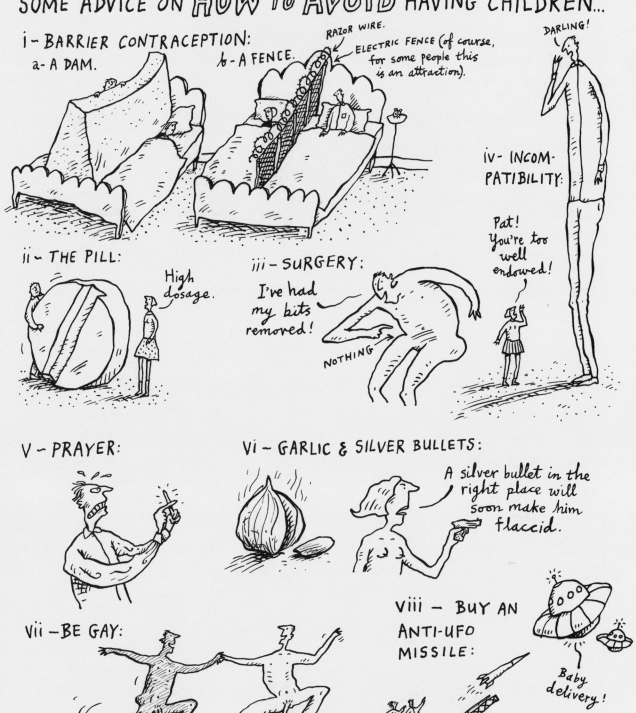

AN INTERACTIVE MOMENT:

You have now reached a crossroads, in life and in this book. It is time to make the decision which will change everything... or not. So – if you have decided to keep your life as it is, choose OPTION A. If you're going to have children, choose OPTION B. (HELPFUL HINT ~ Heads: A. Tails: B).

OPTION A – EXIT BOOK HERE & RETURN IT TO HIGH SHELF.

OPTION B – READ ON...

THE NEXT PHASE:

Congratulations!

Commiserations...

Support stockings.

2
THE NEW ARRIVAL(S)

HOME BIRTH:

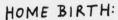

I'll just finish the vacuuming first...

HOSPITAL BIRTH:

...today at Lords...

Waah! Bleep
Bleep Waah!
Waah!
Open wide!
Waaa! Bleep
Bleep

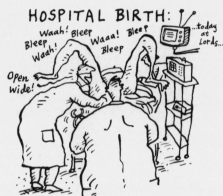

NOT-AT-HOME BIRTH:

She's blocking the aisle.

SALE
FREE!
BARGAINS
Waaa waaaa Waa Waa

WATER BIRTH:

Blub blub blub blub...
PUSH!

AIR BIRTH:

Oops!
Waaaaaaa

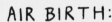

VIRGIN BIRTH:

Gosh! Where on earth did you spring from?!

YAWN...

It is FAR easier to cope with children when you are very young (this is IMPORTANT PIECE OF ADVICE No. 1). If you become a parent in your early twenties you'll breeze through it and still be young enough to go out on the town every night after they've grown up and left home.

For those of you for whom, like me, this advice comes too late, don't despair (that will come later anyway). Just grit your teeth, take a deep breath and HANG ON! It's a nightmare roller coaster ride from which

Hair falling out.

Look! Video arcade, Daddy!

you'll suddenly awaken, around age sixty, and wonder where your life went.

Of course, IMPORTANT PIECE OF ADVICE No. 2 is that cynicism is COMPLETELY the wrong approach to take. Now that your life is over you must make the most of it! Or you'll end up resentful, bitter, grumpy and unlikeable to your partner, friends AND to your children. You'll start staying late at work rather than going home and before you know it you'll be out on your ear and living in the garden.

Instead, glance back briefly at the balmy days of constant sunshine without kids when TIME stretched off into the distance just waiting to be filled with exactly whatever YOU felt like doing at that particular moment.

Once you've said farewell to the past take a deep breath and JUMP UNHESITATINGLY INTO PARENTHOOD WITH BOTH FEET! Whatever you do, DON'T LOOK BACK AGAIN for at LEAST ten years or all around you will turn into a seething pit filled with the writhing snakes of sleeplessness, tidying, washing clothes, cooking, dirty dishes, ironing, bath-time, bedtime, discipline, arguments and punishment.

So LOOK FORWARD, embrace the future and marvellous things happen! The sun comes out and as its rays touch the acres of dirty clothes, mounds of broken toys, videos, half-eaten yoghurts and crisp packets which spread across the sittingroom floor, they magically metamorphose into the magical landscape of childhood.

I looked forward and I'm having fun!

NAUSEATING...

Well I looked back and I turned into a bitter pillar of salt!

SETTLING IN:

i·YOUR NEWLY ARRIVED BABY STILL REMEMBERS HER PAST AND THINKS IN 'ALIEN' – THIS IS WHY BABIES LOOK SO WISE.

Zpple kkk na dk aa tka pt... *

* What planet is this? I hope I remembered to turn off the spaceship lights...

ii·AT TWO MONTHS SHE'S BEGINNING TO ADJUST.

Xxk... pkt... dk luut... *

* Who am I? Where am I?

iii·AT FOUR MONTHS.

Gk... uk... t... *

* I... think... therefore... er...

iv· AND AT SIX MONTHS SHE'S COMPLETELY FORGOTTEN HER OLD LIFE AND IS STARTING TO LEARN HER EARTH LANGUAGE.

Da Da Da! Ma Ma!

A USEFUL GUIDE TO THE DIFFERENT TYPES OF BABY:

The potential variety of babies is virtually infinite. Here are a few of the commonest ones. See if you can find yours.

SWEET & DEAR. FAT. THIN. GIRL. BOY. OTHER.

LOUD. QUIET. WRIGGLY. CUDDLY. UGLY. PRETTY.

BIG. SMALL. BORN WITH TEETH. BORN WITHOUT. WILL TAKE A DUMMY. WON'T.

LONG. SHORT. UPSIDE DOWN. SIDEWAYS. TWINS.

ANGRY. VERY ANGRY. HUNGRY. NOT HUNGRY. TIRED. SMUG.

HOW MUCH HAIR SHOULD A BABY HAVE?

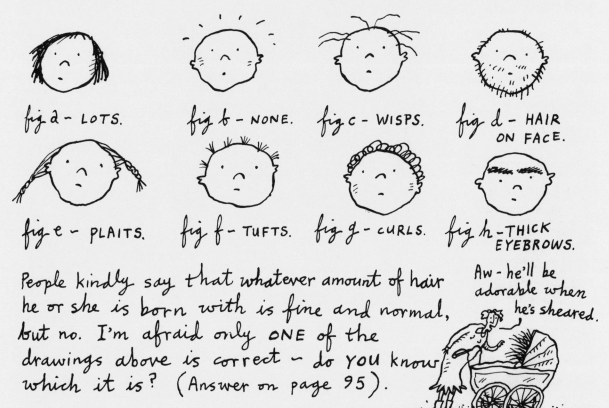

fig a - LOTS.

fig b - NONE.

fig c - WISPS.

fig d - HAIR ON FACE.

fig e - PLAITS.

fig f - TUFTS.

fig g - CURLS.

fig h - THICK EYEBROWS.

People kindly say that whatever amount of hair he or she is born with is fine and normal, but no. I'm afraid only ONE of the drawings above is correct — do YOU know which it is? (Answer on page 95).

Aw — he'll be adorable when he's sheared.

HOW TO TELL YOUR BABY FROM ANOTHER ONE.

Lots of babies look the same, so write your name and phone number on him somewhere unobtrusive with indelible pen.

NO DENTAL RECORDS YET.

3 BABY GAP OUTFITS.

fig a - 3 IDENTICAL BABIES of DIFFERENT PARENTS.

THIS BABY HAS A TATTOO.

TIE ON A TAG.

Why not pop a folded S.A.E. into one of his pockets! Remember to regularly increase the postage as he gets heavier.

19

CHOOSING A NAME

ZEBEDEE; ZORO; ZEKE; ZOWIE...

A useful way to tell babies apart is to give them different names. As part of my plan to make a MILLION, BILLION POUNDS I have COPYRIGHTED every name and will be selling them through my chain of high street outlets.* I'll do special offers on perennial favourites, and I'll hold regular sales when slow-moving names will be heavily discounted.

Today's Special!

BUY "DIANA" & get 1 PETS NAME FREE! 'SPOT' 'BRUNO' etc

I'll take a VERY dim view of any illegal black market names-dealing that I come across. Such activity will be VIGOROUSLY stamped out!

Certain elite names will be released only in expensive, strictly limited editions. It would be wise to put a deposit down to reserve an old family name with sentimental value.

I'm sorry, M'am, but 'Torpmandeville' was strictly an edition of six.

But it was my mother's name!

MAIL ORDER NAME REGISTRATION is available now. Simply fill in the form opposite and post to me, % my publishers.

*Franchises coming soon.

Name registration form

MALE ☐   FEMALE ☐   PET ☐

FIRST CHOICE _____

SECOND CHOICE _____

IF BOTH SELECTIONS UNAVAILABLE, A NAME WILL BE PICKED FROM A HAT.

CHEQUE ☐   POSTAL ORDER ☐   CREDIT CARD No.

YOUR NAME & ADDRESS _____

1 NAME - £45.00! BUY 2 NAMES & GET 'BOB' FREE!!

20

HOW TO HOLD A BABY:

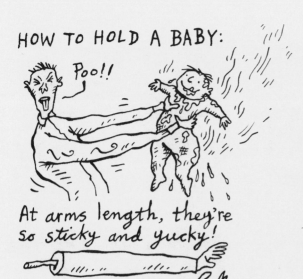

Poo!!

At arms length, they're so sticky and yucky!

↳ Useful arm extensions for VERY dirty babies.

HOW TO BATH A BABY:

You'll need a strap-on APPLEBY EXTRA ARM ™ (or even two!) to hold the baby safely, wash her AND reach for the towel.

DON'T FORGET - too long in the bath and baby will look like a prune:

TOO LONG. →

JUST RIGHT. →

HAIR COMBED. ↖

HOW TO PUT ON A NAPPY:

fold a: fold b: fold c: place tab d onto tab e...   Start again...

TWIST

SOME USEFUL HOLDS:

i - ARMLOCK: ii - KNEE PRESS:

HURRAH! IT'S DONE!!

The FLYING DUTCHMAN.
↙ For variety, try origami nappy folding. I particularly like the APOCALYPSE.

of course, all parents are obsessed by poo colour and consistency. Turn to page 33 for a useful chart.

21

FEEDING

fig a ~ THE TWO FOOD CUPBOARDS:

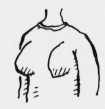

POSITION i -   POSITION ii -   POSITION iii -

MOVING ON TO SOLID FOOD:

This is easy. The manufacturers have done all the hard work. All you have to do is spoon it in.

PIE & CHIPS.   MASH & SAUSAGE.   BACON SAUSAGE 2 EGGS TOMS & A FRIED SLICE.   COD & CHIPS.   HADDOCK & CHIPS WITH PEAS, 2 SLICES AND A MUG OF TEA.   ICED DONUT, BISCUITS, CAKE & FIZZY POP.   a.   b.   c.

(HANDY HINT - they'll usually eat it cold!)

FINGER FOOD:

CHIPS.   BISCUIT.   CAKE.   CHOCOLATE.   LOLLY.   SOIL.

It gives baby a sense of achievement to feed himself and is character building - he'll have the confidence to leave home earlier when he's older.

SUBMERGED ROCKS!

While you're plain sailing (above) don't flounder on the rock of keeping your designer outfit clean! Here are two suggestions to prevent soiling yourself...

POLO NECK.   VELCRO FLAP for MOBILE PHONE access.

Try a PARENT BIB with arms...

COME TO DADDY!

or a PROTECTIVE FEEDING AND CUDDLING SUIT.

a salutary story...
THE PERIL OF CALLING BABIES PET NAMES BASED ON FOOD!

"Hello, Honey Pie!"

"You funny little sausage."

"My sweet little pork chop!"

"You wee crusty dumpling."

"Butterball..."

"Potato Cake..."

"Angel Cake..."

"Naughty little Scampi..."

"Current Bun..."

"My little biscuit."

"Nugget..."

"Fruit flan..."

"Jammy donut..."

"Bean..."

"You darling wee Pudding-in-a-basin."

AN UNFORTUNATE ACCIDENT:

Would you like a biscuit, Mrs Smitherington?

Oh dear...

I've already helped myself to the big, fat, Jammy one, thank you Edna.

BELCH!

23

NIGHT TIME ~ THE BABY CLOCK.

THE MANY MOODS of SLEEP DEPRIVATION...

STILL COULD BE OKAY · HOPE · OPTIMISM · RESIGNATION... · GLOOM · HOPELESSNESS · DESPAIR – make appointment for counselling. · DEPRESSION

Darling! I'm off to work and the septuplets have just woken up...

SOME SUGGESTIONS FOR TRAINING YOUR BABY TO SLEEP THROUGH THE NIGHT:

i ~ Treat baby like an adult.   ii ~ Treat baby like a budgie.

Want to go to bed yet? Maybe after 'Newsnight'?

COT COVER

That'll keep her quiet!

24

OR... WHY NOT TRY HAVING YOUR BABY SLEEP IN BED WITH YOU? It's easier than getting up for each breastfeed, battle of wills, etc. You'll notice, however, that in the wee small hours babies aquire GIANT proportions...

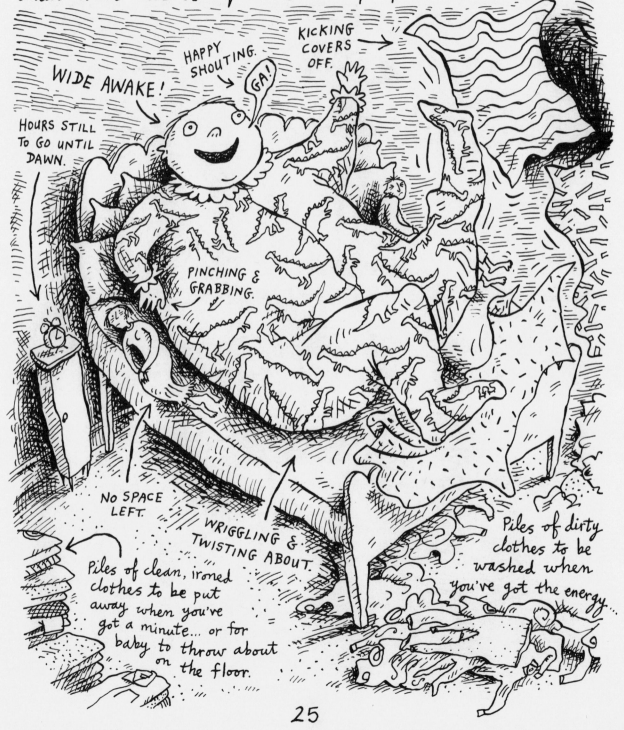

SOME LAWS OF BABY BEHAVIOUR

i – They exude drool, dribble and a strange, sticky slime.

ii – They will cry in a car seat and in a hat.

iii – They will suck your nose...

iv – And squeeze your lips too hard.

V – They will empty a box.

vi – If you sit them up they will fall over and hit the back of their heads.

vii – They will stand up under a table.

viii – They will break your glasses.

ix – They will learn to roll over the minute you leave them for a split second on a bed or on a sofa.

It's never too soon to BEGIN YOUR CHILD'S EDUCATION!
Give your baby a head start with these cut-out FLASH CARDS:

MY FAVOURITE CARTOONIST IS STEVEN APPLEBY

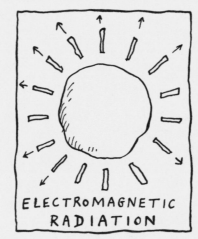

ELECTROMAGNETIC RADIATION

EUATHLUS EMILIA.
(MEXICAN TARANTULA)

H₂O

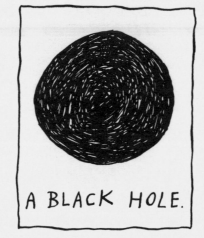

A BLACK HOLE.

I AM DEVELOPING AN OEDIPUS COMPLEX.

MY FAVOURITE AUTHOR IS WILL SELF

DON'T WORRY if your baby isn't born yet. You can still get him or her started by shouting out the alphabet, numbers one to ten and some simple spelling and sums while baby is still in the womb.

2+2=4

29

OF COURSE, **EVERY PARENT** THINKS THEIR OWN BABY IS **PERFECT** AND WANTS TO **SHOW HIM OFF...**

A WARNING!

LET THIS <u>TRUE</u> <u>EXPERIENCE</u> ALERT DADS EVERYWHERE TO THE FACT THAT HAVING A BABY ISN'T ALL GOOEY SENTIMENTALITY...

IT'S SWEET TO SEE HOW EARLY A BABY LEARNS TO TELL THE DIFFERENCE BETWEEN MUM & DAD.

A USEFUL DIAGNOSTIC REFERENCE CHART of POO:

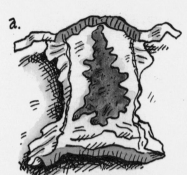

a. DISGUSTING! This is a normal, healthy baby.

b. No cause for SERIOUS concern — YET...

c. 2 pennies and a marble. Keep an eye out for the £1 you lost.

d. You put your nappy on the rabbit by mistake. Go and rescue your baby from the rabbit hutch.

e. Rain tomorrow — remember to take the pram cover.

f. You will come into money... so enter the lottery. In fact, better leave the baby next door and run up to the lottery shop NOW!

g. The profile of the person you SHOULD have married.

h. Next week's winning lottery numbers. RUN back up to the lottery shop <u>IMMEDIATELY!</u>

i. This appears to be an amused nappy... What it finds amusing, I cannot imagine.

FOUR EXAMPLES *of* NAPPY RASH:

a – THE CATHERINE WHEEL:

b – DOGFIGHT OVER DIEPPE:

c – THE LAUGHING POLICEMAN:

d – AUSTRALIA:

Next time YOUR baby has nappy rash count how many different pictures you can see.

SOME WORRYING SNOT COLOURS:

a –

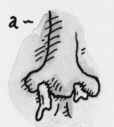

TRANSPARENT.

b –

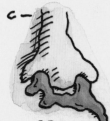

YELLOW.

c –

GREEN.

d –

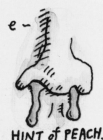

MAGNOLIA.

e –

HINT *of* PEACH.

f –

SMALL PIECE *of* LONG-LOST LEGO.

g –

LARGE PIECE *of* LONG-LOST LEGO.

h –

THIS ISN'T SNOT, IT'S CHOCOLATE.

i –

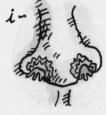

CRUSTY.

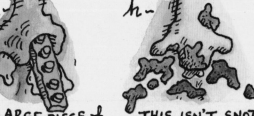

34

SOME **VOMIT** TO WATCH OUT FOR:

GREEN

Oops!   My nice new Jumper!

BLEAH...

BANANA, CHOCOLATE, SOIL, VARIOUS PLANT LEAVES & CHEWED SNAIL.

RESISTANT TO ALL KNOWN BIOLOGICAL CLEANERS AND STAIN REMOVERS.

RED

ORGANIC BEETROOT, BLOOD PUDDING & BLACKCURRANT BABY DINNER ON CREAM LINEN SUIT.

BLEAH!

DRY CLEAN FIRST, THEN TRY BOIL WASH. TRY BOIL WASH AGAIN, THEN FLING GARMENT IN BIN.

OTHER...

VIRTUALLY ANYTHING ON A BRAND NEW WHITE SILK BLOUSE.

DON'T EVEN BOTHER TO UNWRAP IT. JUST THROW GARMENT STRAIGHT INTO BIN.

HOW TO **READ** YOUR BABY'S **MIND!**

Work out what he's thinking by comparing these colour swatches to his face:

"I love you, Mummy."

"Okay, that's enough of that."

"I'm starving!"

"Now I feel a bit queasy."

"I am UTTERLY FURIOUS! I found that very old crust!!"

 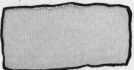  

"And HOW DARE YOU TAKE THAT TINY, DANGEROUS THING OUT OF MY MOUTH!!"

"Now, where's my marble gone? Did you take THAT too?!!"

"HELP! HELP! I'm CHOKING! I've found the marble and it's STUCK IN MY THROAT..."

"Thank you. That's better... aha! There's a five pence piece..."

THE 'BASTILLE'
designer French
play pen:

THE LOOK-BUT-
DON'T-TOUCH
baby training
cupboard, with
toughened glass inner door.

THE REVOLVING FLOOR
& MOVING CRAWL-WAY
returns a crawling
baby to its starting
point automatically.

Almost silent.

Buzz... CLUNK!

clank...

rattle

HUM

KACHUNK

BONK!

THE WATER-FREE SAFETY BATH:
Baby can be left unattended
without fear of drowning,
banging head or escaping.
Save on soap and towels!
(Lid available).

PADDED
WALLS.

FLOOR STAYS
DRY.

FINALLY, it's never too soon
to give baby some responsibility.
Try this CAR SEAT with
REAL WORKING steering wheel!

No! No!
Aaargh!!

Goo goo
gah...

SMASH!

TEACH YOUR KIDS WITH *Steven Appleby's* **MUTANT ANIMALS** COUNTING **BOOK**

A COW WITH **1** LEG.

moo!

A PIG WITH **2** HEADS.

OINK

A DUCK WITH **3** BEAKS.

A BIRD WITH **4** WINGS.

A FISH WITH **5** EYES.

SOME BABY ADVICE

CHANGING THE BABY.

I'd like to exchange this baby for another one.

ALWAYS WEAR THE PROTECTIVE GOGGLES.

Hello, Clement... NAPPY TIME!

REMEMBER TO WASH YOUR HANDS AFTER TOUCHING A BABY.

Yuk!

USEFUL WORDS TO SAY TO YOUR BABY.

NO!
STOP THAT!
DON'T TOUCH!

WRITE DOWN ALL THOSE FUNNY LITTLE THINGS HE SAYS IN A BABY BOOK.

His first words! "Earthling, this is your race's final warning!" Adorable.

BE PREPARED TO LET GO OF THE REINS.

Off you go out into the wide world. I won't hold you back. Just be happy...

3
GROWING PAINS...

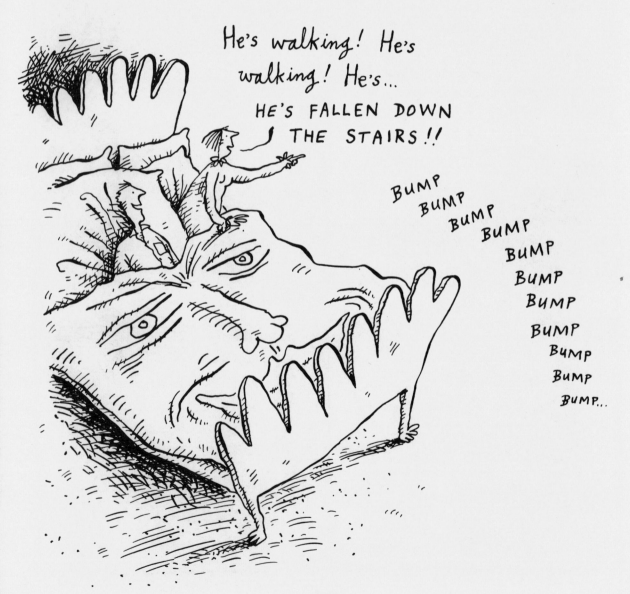

Suddenly one morning you wake up and you've got a TODDLER!

He's walking! He's walking! He's...

HE'S FALLEN DOWN THE STAIRS!!

BUMP
BUMP
BUMP
BUMP
BUMP
BUMP
BUMP
BUMP
BUMP
BUMP
BUMP...

THE 12 BASIC TYPES OF TODDLER.

LEARNING TO TALK

Now that your child is a toddler, his baby repertoire of MUM, DAD and CAT will soon be joined by new words like NO, WON'T, CAN'T, DON'T and NEVER. Next he'll be putting them together into sentences and in no time you'll be fully interacting with him. Here are 3 examples:

43

TODDLER EATING HABITS:

SOME TODDLER EATING DISORDERS:

SCURVY — caused by living on junk food.

MALNUTRITION — This girl is the daughter of new-age vegetarians.

TOO MUCH ENERGY — IT CAN'T BE NORMAL! Too much fizzy pop and sweets.

ONE OF THOSE TYPICAL AWKWARD QUESTIONS ABOUT FOOD WHICH CHILDREN ASK:

Which chip is the leader?

LEARNING the TRUTH about the WORLD can be...

i - PAINFUL:

ii - CONFUSING:

HERE ARE SOME HARMLESS LIES TO TELL YOUR CHILDREN...

45

LEARNING THROUGH PLAY - LET'S PRETEND...

WHAT TO SAY TO _YOUR_ TODDLER TO GIVE COMFORT & HELP...

When he's feeling a bit unwell - maybe with cramp or a tummy ache:

Stop making such a fuss!

When he's suffering from NIGHT FEARS or other phobias:

Oh, don't be so silly!

When he's feeling shy:

Come on! Pull yourself together!

When she's learning to read:

HORSEY!

Oh, for goodness sake you're just not trying!

When he's starting to use a potty:

For Pete's sake it isn't exactly difficult!!

When she's learning how to ride a bike:

I could ride NO HANDS when I was your age!

PLEASE PLEASE PLEASE...

Saying 'PLEASE' is the holy grail of bringing up children successfully. This one word is the foundation upon which the entire colossal, tottering edifice of LIFE is built. Without it the wobbling tower of school, friendships, relationships, marriage, work, unemployment, middle age, retirement and, ultimately, death, collapses — crushing you in the rubble.

Here are some of the CODES parents use to jog their youngsters' minds:

fig a-
What's the magic word?

fig b-
I'm WAITING...

fig c-
YES?

AN EXAMPLE OF 'PLEASE' IN ACTION:
Take me to your leader, earthling!

NEVER!

Please please please...

Oh, Alright.

THE **TRAGIC** RESULT OF **FAILING** TO TRAIN YOUR FAMILY THOROUGHLY!

REMEMBER! ALWAYS SET STRICT BOUNDARIES...

Oh no - she's HAVING A TANTRUM!

Tantrums usually start when children become toddlers and they can continue for years. Just look at these distressing examples...

fig a: THREE YEARS OLD.

WANT BALLOON!

WANT RED! NOT BLUE!!

WAAAAAAAAAH!! WANT RED!

STAMP!

Aww... Daddy will get you another balloon!

I WAAAAAAAAAAAH!!

LATER...

PAT!

Daddy drove to the shop and got you this red one!

?

DON'T WANT RED! WANT YELLOW!!

WAAA... -AAAA... AAAA... AAH!!

fig b: THIRTY-THREE YEARS OLD.

AAARGH!!! RIGHT!! THAT'S IT!! I'VE HAD IT!! GET UP TO BED THIS INSTANT! NOW! WITHOUT ANY SUPPER, BREAKFAST, STORY, LUNCH, TEA... RANT! RAVE!

Calm down, darling! You'll do yourself a mischief...

Sssh...

Think of the neighbours...

STAMP!

HOW TO HOLD A CONVERSATION WITH SMALL CHILDREN AROUND:

i ~ At last! We can have a conversation now that I've sent him out of the room.

I'm back, Daddy!

ii – WAIT UNTIL THE CHILDREN HAVE GONE TO BED:

what were we going to talk about?... YAWN...

I'm not tired, Daddy!

HOP! JUMP!

iii – HAVE A CONVERSATION WHICH IS EASY TO FOLLOW:

Nice day.   Yes.

SING ME A SONG, MUMMY! WHERE MY BIKE, DADDY! LOOK, A BIRDIE!

iv – USE A DISTRACTION TECHNIQUE:

Look! An aeroplane!
   "And THEN he said..."
Look! A fire engine!
   "I've met someone else and I'm leaving you..."
Look! A Robin Redbreast!
   "So she took the kitchen knife and..."
Look! A froggie!

GOSH...

v – BE FIRM:

Don't interrupt when I'm talking!

↑ A HOPELESS APPROACH ALWAYS DOOMED TO FAILURE.

I'm an alien, Dad!

REMEMBER... as your children get older
THEY WON'T LISTEN TO A <u>WORD</u> YOU SAY...

Breakfast time!

Time to get dressed!

SCHOOLTIME! Let's go!!

Feed the rabbits!

Tidy your rooms!

Have you done your homework?

THE ENEMY.

TURN THAT T.V. OFF!

DO YOUR CHORES!!

...UNLESS YOU GET <u>REALLY</u> ANGRY!!

BEDTIME!!

Cool it, Mum!

No need to shout...

Yeah.

IF ALL ELSE FAILS, YOU CAN ALWAYS DRAW ON YOUR ULTIMATE SECRET WEAPON:

BOO HOO HOO...

You lot NEVER do what I ask!

SOB SNIFF...

Just going to tidy up!

Feed the rabbits!

Help!

The SEPTUPLETS' first trip to Babyland.
You must be so proud!
Aw.. sweet!
I'd like seven prams, please, and seven cots, seven car seats, seven high chairs, seven wind-up mobiles, seven baby bouncers, seven back packs, seven dummies, seven bottles, seven...
SALE STARTS TOMORROW!
MOBILE
MOBILE
MOBILE
MOBILE
MOBILE
MOBILE
MOBILE
BUY SEVEN PRAMS & GET 1 FREE!
BULK BU
DISCOU

The SEPTUPLETS bake cakes.

4

SOME SAFETY ADVICE

AND DON'T FORGET TO STOP YOUR CHILDREN DOING ALL THOSE <u>FUN AND DANGEROUS THINGS</u> YOU USED TO DO WHEN YOU WERE A KID!

(Whatever you do, DON'T send your kids to stay with their Grandparents!!)

5
KNOWING WHEN TO STOP!

How many is enough? Why not stop RIGHT NOW at whatever number of children you have accumulated? It will probably be the right decision. However, if you are unsure about whether to pick up the phone and book your husband's vasectomy, take a moment to glance over the information below:

Fig 1 - THIS GRAPH SHOWS HOW AGING ACCELERATES IN DIRECT PROPORTION TO THE NUMBER OF CHILDREN YOU HAVE:

Fig 2 - SOME EXAMPLES OF HOW FORGETFULNESS INCREASES WITH NUMBER OF CHILDREN:

1 CHILD - Parents can remember child's name 100% of the time.

2 CHILDREN - 90%

4 CHILDREN - 65%

5 CHILDREN - 40%

6 CHILDREN - Er... what point was I trying to make?..

Fig 3 - INCOME OF NANNY RELATIVE TO BOTH PARENTS:

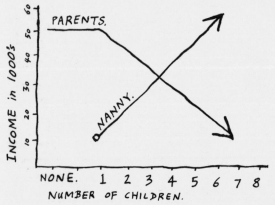

Fig 4 - THE REASON WHY:

Haha! My ray gun is ageing the earthling and sucking out her thoughts!

DINNER TIME!.. Er, what's-his-name...

6

THE ARRIVAL OF SCHOOLDAYS

TEACHERS PET:

UNUSUAL & FUNNY NAMES

IF YOUR CHILD IS BEING TEASED AT SCHOOL, COULD THIS BE THE REASON WHY?*

* Worried about permanent psychological damage to little Niagara Poot Bobbin? Turn to page 20 and change her to Doris immediately!

Extracts from:
A MODERN SCHOOL TEXTBOOK

MAKING NEW FRIENDS

~ HERE ARE SOME TYPICAL CHILDREN OF THE SORT YOUR CHILD WILL MEET IN HIS OR HER CLASS:

A BOY WITH SPECIAL POWERS:

I can see through walls...

A PSYCHOPATH:

Come on!

After you!

A SUPER BRAINY GIRL:

Girls just ARE brainier than boys.

A CLAIRVOYANT GIRL:

Don't fly on a plane, or... UGH!

A SENSITIVE & SHY TYPE:

AN OUT-GOING TYPE:

Come on - let's go out!

But we just got to school!!

AN UNSUITABLE SCHOOL FRIEND:

I don't like you!

Give me your lunch... NOW!!

UNSUITABLE INVISIBLE FRIENDS:

Your father and I don't like you associating with THAT sort of invisible friend!

A SPOON BENDER:

Oops...

Don't invite HER again!

THE BENEFITS of your children going to school, aside from their getting an education, are obvious...

Try to choose a school with lots of extra-curricular activities stretching away into the evening. Persuade her to join the choir and enrole him in the Warhammer roleplaying game society. Of course, you could go private, but it's expensive and you have to weigh up the advantage of school on Saturday morning against the disadvantage of longer holidays. Boarding school gets them out of the way for weeks on end, but it needs great resolve to ignore their constant pleading to come home. Remember – it's just attention seeking.

SUDDENLY ALONG COME THE HOLIDAYS!

There's a bill going through Parliament which will reduce school holidays to a couple of days at Christmas and a morning at Easter. But until then...

Come on! Don't watch T.V. all day! Do something else!!

Okay, mum, we'll...

DRAW ALL OVER THE WALLS:

Aargh!

EMPTY ALL THE TOY BOXES ONTO THE FLOOR:

I've made a mountain!

RUN WATER THROUGH THE CEILING:

Stop brushing your teeth!

PLAY WITH MATCHES:

I'm lighting the electric fire, Mum!

RIGHT! I'VE got some suggestions for you!!

Take a look at the next page...

SOME FUN & CREATIVE THINGS TO DO

WHICH WILL KEEP CHILDREN OCCUPIED ON HOLIDAY...

HERE'S A SMART BALLOON SUIT:

I'm going to pop myself!

WHY NOT ENCOURAGE THEM TO TAKE UP SWORD SWALLOWING?

Your Mum said you'd like it!

SWORD SWALLOWING KIT

WITH REAL SWORD!

OUCH!

THIS FIREWORK OUTFIT WILL APPEAL TO ALL AGES:

Just light the blue touchpaper!

ROMAN CANDLE

HOW ABOUT MAKING YOUR 6 YEAR OLD A HEDGEHOG SUIT?

Be careful crossing the road, dear!

HERE'S A USEFUL DIG-YOUR-OWN-GRAVE SET (complete with spade and tombstone).

YOUR NAME & DATES GO HERE.

R.I.P.

EDUCATIONAL & FUN! DIG YOUR GRAVE

WATCH OUT FOR THESE
COMMON CHILDHOOD ILLNESSES...

HERE'S <u>ONE WAY</u> to treat an outbreak of I'M BORED...

I'm BORED!

What shall I do now?

I'm BORED...

Come on, children!

IT'S TIME TO DO YOUR CHORES

As soon as children are old enough to go to school they are old enough to do chores. In fact, some say they are ready even earlier, but despite the cheering legends passed from parent to parent concerning children age 4 who can vacuum the house or do the washing and ironing, my personal experience suggests that at 4 – or even 5 – they are too small to reach the washing machine controls safely. Standing them on a chair or box to do the ironing is asking for trouble too. You don't want a burn on that favourite designer polo-neck boob tube now do you!

The best way to get chirpy children cheerfully completing chores is to pay them – which needn't be as sordid as it sounds. How about a sweet currency?
5 CHEWS = 1 LOLLIPOP
5 LOLLIPOPS = 1 GIANT-CHOC CHIP ICE CREAM CONE.

You must be joking, Mum!

LET'S SEE HOW IT WORKS ELSEWHERE...

On our planet the children do <u>ALL</u> the household chores while the adults do nothing!

DON'T LIKE FISH!

Eat up or <u>NO PUDDING</u>, Dad!

80

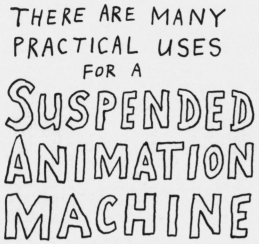

The last resort:
THE CHILDREN ARE SOLD INTO SLAVERY.

AAAAAARGH!

8 SOUND OF DIALING AS THEY RING FRIENDS.

WEET
BLOOP
BLEEP
BAAA
DEET
DEET
DOOO
DOOO...

9 CLUMP! CLUMP! CLUMP! OF FEET ON STAIRS WHEN ASKED TO PLEASE BE QUIET.

10 SLAM OF BEDROOM DOOR WHEN TOLD THEY ARE TOO TIRED TO STAY UP AND WATCH LATE, LATE HORROR FILM.

11 MOANS OF COMPLAINT WHEN ASKED TO HELP SET THE TABLE.

Awww!

CRASH!

12 MUTTERING UNDER BREATH WHEN ACCUSED OF TREATING PARENTS AS SLAVES.

I heard that!

13 SCREAMS OF PAIN WHEN BARELY TOUCHED. HONESTLY!

GOSH!
OW!
YOW!
OUCH!
OH!

14 CLICKS, TAPS, WHISTLES, RATTLING, SINGING, HUMMING, DRUMMING, ETC. AT DINNER TABLE.

CLUNK! OF A PIN DROPPING WHEN ASKED HOW SCHOOL WENT AND DO YOU HAVE A GIRLFRIEND YET?

BA-DOOM!!

BOUNCE

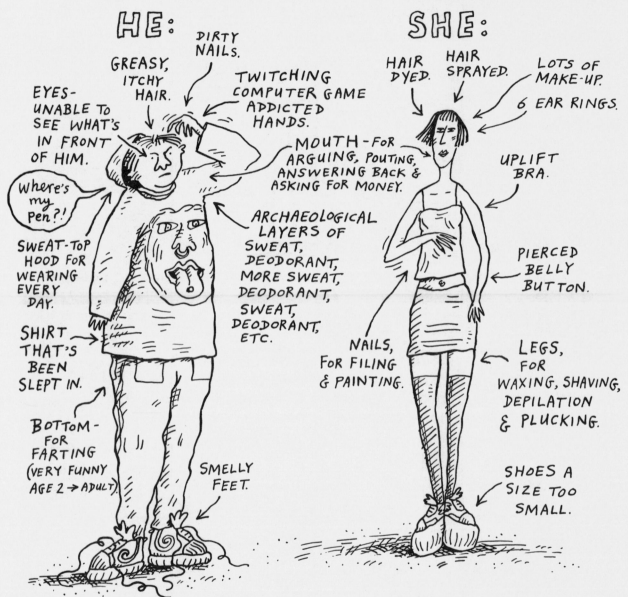

AND NOW — A TEENAGER'S ANATOMY

HE:

GREASY, ITCHY HAIR.

DIRTY NAILS.

TWITCHING COMPUTER GAME ADDICTED HANDS.

EYES - UNABLE TO SEE WHAT'S IN FRONT OF HIM.

Where's my pen?!

SWEAT-TOP HOOD FOR WEARING EVERY DAY.

MOUTH - FOR ARGUING, POUTING, ANSWERING BACK & ASKING FOR MONEY.

ARCHAEOLOGICAL LAYERS OF SWEAT, DEODORANT, MORE SWEAT, DEODORANT, SWEAT, DEODORANT, ETC.

SHIRT THAT'S BEEN SLEPT IN.

BOTTOM - FOR FARTING (VERY FUNNY AGE 2 → ADULT)

SMELLY FEET.

SHE:

HAIR DYED.

HAIR SPRAYED.

LOTS OF MAKE-UP.

6 EAR RINGS.

UPLIFT BRA.

PIERCED BELLY BUTTON.

NAILS, FOR FILING & PAINTING.

LEGS, FOR WAXING, SHAVING, DEPILATION & PLUCKING.

SHOES A SIZE TOO SMALL.

HABITS:
Rarely seen in the bathroom.
Pretends not to be interested in girls.
Polite to all except parents.
Flounces about & sulks.

HABITS:
Always in the bathroom.
Constantly writing in diary.
Tries on entire wardrobe before dressing.
Flounces about & sulks.

AN UP-TO-THE-MINUTE GUIDE TO THE LATEST TEENAGE FASHIONS AND SLANG!

To keep this page up to date, SPY on your teenagers and LISTEN IN to their conversations (a telephone extension is ideal) then fill in the blank sections below. Use a pencil so that you can rub it out and update the page every few months.

USE THESE TWO FIGURE OUTLINES to sketch in clothing, hairstyles, tattoos, body piercings, cosmetic surgery and other visual changes

MALE.

FEMALE (or vice versa).

SLANG WORDS:	MEANING:	CONTEXT:
1 _ _ _ _ _ _ _ _	_ _ _ _ _ _	_ _ _ _ _ _ _ _ _
2 _ _ _ _ _ _ _ _	_ _ _ _ _ _	_ _ _ _ _ _ _ _ _
3 _ _ _ _ _ _ _ _	_ _ _ _ _ _	_ _ _ _ _ _ _ _ _
4 _ _ _ _ _ _ _ _	_ _ _ _ _ _	_ _ _ _ _ _ _ _ _
5 _ _ _ _ _ _ _ _	_ _ _ _ _ _	_ _ _ _ _ _ _ _ _
6 _ _ _ _ _ _ _ _	_ _ _ _ _ _	_ _ _ _ _ _ _ _ _
7 _ _ _ _ _ _ _ _	_ _ _ _ _ _	_ _ _ _ _ _ _ _ _

THINGS YOU NEVER THOUGHT YOU'D HEAR YOURSELF SAYING!

PARENTS ARE EMBARRASSING...

Teenagers don't like having their early baby boobs and toddler faux pas brought up at the dinner table.

Of course, as every parent knows, lying in bed is part of the larvae stage every teenager goes through before their metamorphosis from a strange alien creature into an adult human being.

SOME VIEWS OF THE DUVET STAGE:

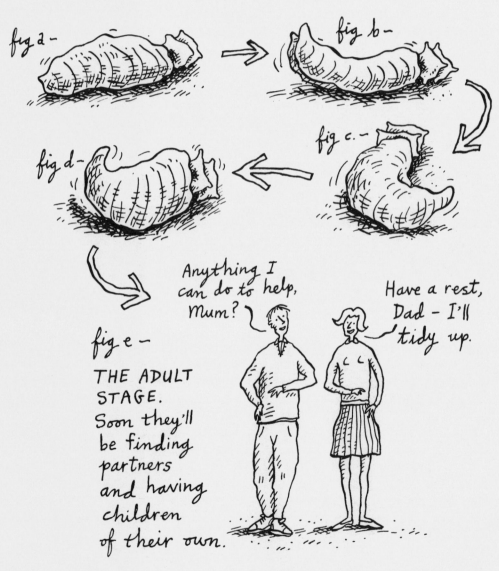

fig a –

fig b –

fig c. –

fig d –

fig e –

THE ADULT STAGE.
Soon they'll be finding partners and having children of their own.

Anything I can do to help, Mum?

Have a rest, Dad – I'll tidy up.

The Motto of this Book:

INVEST IN YOUR CHILDREN AND THEY WILL
REPAY YOU A THOUSANDFOLD.

I'm going to invest
my children in a
building society.

INDEX